Patio and Kit
Gard

A Beginner's Guide to 21 Herbs You Can Grow at Home

by Julia Winchester

First Published in 2013 by Cardigan River LLC
Copyright © 2013 Julia Winchester
Photo credits: Cover: © Tim Scott - Fotolia.com
ISBN 10: 0988443376
ISBN 13: 978-0-9884433-7-2

Disclaimer

No part of this publication may be reproduced or transmitted in any form or by any means, mechanical or electronic, including photocopying or recording, or by any information storage and retrieval system, or transmitted by email without permission in writing from the publisher.

While all attempts have been made to verify the information provided in this publication, neither the author nor the publisher assumes any responsibility for errors, omissions, or contrary interpretations of the subject matter herein.

This book is for educational purposes only. The publisher and authors of this instructional book are not responsible in any manner whatsoever for any adverse effects arising directly or indirectly as a result of the information provided in this book. The views expressed are those of the author alone, and should not be taken as expert instruction or commands. The use of any information provided in this book is solely at your own risk.

Adherence to all applicable laws and regulations, including international, federal, state and local governing professional licensing, business practices, advertising, and all other aspects of doing business in the US, Canada or any other jurisdiction is the sole responsibility of the purchaser or reader.

Any perceived slight of any individual or organization is purely unintentional.

Table of Contents

Chapter 1: Introduction

Why Grow Herbs?

Wouldn't it be great if you could reach over to your windowsill, grab some freshly grown herbs, toss them into a pan to flavor your dish with flare and then to serve them to your guests? Sure, you would have incredible flavor and all kinds of healthy nutrients, but you would look like a superstar chef! Who doesn't want that?

Growing herbs at home, whether on a patio, windowsill, or even the balcony of your apartment is a real option. In fact, it is one of the best ways for you to finally get the nutrients your body needs with the flavor you are craving. Why do it? Why put the time and money into growing them from scratch or even just growing plants like this? Just consider a few of the main reasons so many are using this method to get the herbs they want and need.

It's Space Saving at Its Best

One of the main reasons to grow herbs in the kitchen or on the patio is because it is one of the most convenient options available. In an urban setting, you may not have a lot of room to spread out. You may not have a plot of land in the backyard to create an incredible garden out of. This is a common problem.

- You don't have access to green space.

- You don't want to dig up your garden or yard to make room for a garden.

- You simply do not want to spend your time on your hands and knees digging through weeds.

- You are not allowed to dig - it's a condo or a rental home.

- There's not enough sunlight for direct plant growth.

However, you want the benefits that can come from access to herbs for your meals. Using a small space in your apartment, condo, or even your home, you can create exactly what you want in terms of quality herbs.

In fact, all you need is a small amount of space like the sill. Depending on how many plants you wish to grow and the type, you may only need a few individualized pots to hold each of the herbs you hope to grow. As long as you can place this by the windowsill or in an area where there is ample direct sunlight, you have all of the space you need for a fantastic growing garden.

It's Economical

You could do what many people are doing to get fresh herbs. They buy packages of them in the grocery store. Those packages come with four or five leaves of the fresh herb. The problem is, that little package can also cost you $5 to $8. That means for one pasta dish, you may spend more on the herbs than the pasta and the sauce combined. It just does not make sense especially if you want to have access to the finest herbs on a regular basis.

It's frugal, on the other hand, to invest in some quality pots and soil and grow your own. Though you will need to learn how to do this, it takes just a few minutes of your time to set it up and to put this in place. Once the plants begin to grow, you'll have no limitation on the access you have to the herbs you want to enjoy.

You can easily step over to the window, harvest a few leaves, add them to a dish, and enjoy them. There's no worry about not having something in hand. Even better, you can control how much you grow. Though you may have to replant from time to time, especially if you are planning to be a heavy user of herbs, you'll find that it will cost you probably $10 to $20 one time to have continuously available herbs at your disposal. Is there any reason to put off this process any longer? It will save you money in the long term.

It Could Be Better for You

When you plant and grow your own herbs, you are able to control every element in them. That means you can select organic soils and seeds. You choose if you need to add pesticides or fertilizers, preferably natural and organic choices since the option is yours. That means you do not have to worry about what's on the herbs you are consuming.

Think about this. If you've ever purchased those plastic containers of herbs with a few leaves in them, have you ever noticed that they tend to last for several days even up to a week? Now, if you went into your garden and picked a few leaves from a plant, would they really last that long? Not likely. This is a key indication that there are chemicals or products added to these leaves to keep them looking good for days after they are picked.

This can also indicate that there is a reduced level of nutrition in herbs. As you will learn, there are many reasons to invest in herbs grown fresh. However, if you are buying prepackaged products, including anything that's frozen, canned, or dried, you are not going to get the highest concentration of nutrients you need and deserve. That's a big problem. Rather, you'll get poor levels of the nutrients you need.

Depending on the type of herb you buy, you could be getting a very rich level of nutrients. Herbs may contain:

- An assortment of vitamins

- Numerous minerals your body needs

- High antioxidant levels which are good for fighting toxins in the body

This can help you to fight off illness, boost your overall health, and even help you to sharpen your mental abilities. When it comes down to it, herbs are good for you. You may even be able to use them as an herbal remedy. Perhaps you want to tap into them to help you to fight off a cold. You can use them to help with infections, too. The bottom line is that herbs - in their fresh state - are very good for you.

It's Visually Stimulating

If you are still looking for a reason for why you should incorporate an herb garden on your porch or window, just think of all of the dishes you'll be motivated to make when those herbs are just sitting there ready for your use.

- Perhaps you'll be motivated to create a fresh salad with vibrant greens.

- Maybe you'll get motivated to make fresh sauce from scratch using basil and parsley.

- You may be able to make a wonderful fish dish that you've loved for years that doesn't taste good without the use of fresh herbs.

- Do you love Mexican food but hate to spend too much on cilantro?

- Maybe adding a peppermint to your favorite hot chocolate mix is exactly what you need on a cold day.

There's no limit to what you can make. With a full garden of your favorite herbs sitting there just waiting for you to use them, you'll be able to add them right in. You may even want to plan your menu around what's fresh and available to you. It's definitely easy to do when everything is right there on hand.

Now is the perfect time to get started, too. Everything you need is readily available. You'll find an assortment of options available to choose from so you can have the specific types of herbs you want. Roll up your sleeves, grab a bag of soil, and start planting. In a short amount of time, you'll have a fantastic meal in front of you, seasoned not with salt, but with fresh herbs you grew from scratch.

Chapter 2: Preparation for At-Home Growth

Are you ready to take the plunge? Perhaps you are excited to get started. You should be. Soon, your home will smell good and your dishes will taste wonderfully. The question is, though, where do you start? It may not be as difficult as you think.

Before you begin buying anything or getting any seeds started, it's important to do some prep work. You'll need to consider a variety of factors to ensure that the environment you've selected is going to be ideal for growth of your plants.

One of the first things to do is to consider what you would like to grow. Later in this book, we will discuss the actual process as well as pinpoint some very specific plants to consider based on your experience and the amount of work you need to do. However, in this step, we want to keep things a bit more broad. In other words, these are the basic conditions you'll need in order to be successful at growing herbs indoors.

Location, Location, Location

Like with real estate, location is still everything. Obviously, if you pick a dark corner of your home, the plants will not even sprout. If, on the other hand, you select an area with ample light, your chances of seeing seedlings grow are very good. There are some specific things to keep in mind as you consider these options, though.

Light

It seems like a no-brainer to turn to the kitchen as your spot to grow herbs. It may be just that. However, most kitchens are lit by the big light bulb in the ceiling rather than the sun in the sky. In other words, most lack enough sunlight to provide you with the necessary light to grow. That is a problem. Though each plant's needs are different, most will require at least some direct sunlight throughout the course of the day to grow.

- In the morning, note when the entire window is lit up by sunlight. Pick any day or any window you hope to use. Jot down the time.

- Later in the day, when the afternoon is approaching, watch the window again. When is the sunlight reduced? When do you notice that the light is not as bright? Jot that number down as well.

Most plants benefit from at least 6 to 12 hours of direct sunlight each day. What you may notice is that your kitchen window isn't ideal any longer. Look for light that's as direct as possible. While you may think herbs have to be in the kitchen, they can be a beautiful, decorative element to any room of the home. They are even great in terms of refreshing the air. Pick the area of your home with the most sunlight.

Is Natural or Artificial Light Best?

There is no doubt that having natural light sources for your plants are going to be best. It's natural, after all, which means it is giving plants exactly the nutrients they need. However, don't give up on window gardening altogether because the light source you have isn't the sun. In other words, you'll want to consider the use of artificial lighting.

A traditional light bulb may not be effective. Rather, look for a growth light if at all possible. This will give you the best overall circumstances since it produces heat as well as light for your plants. These do not have to be expensive, but they may be vital in some areas when you need additional light.

Think Patio

If possible, step outdoors at least a little bit. The best place for your herbs to grow is going to be outdoors. You may not have land to plant in, but you may still have an outdoor space to use.

- Patios are great when they have some shelter from the elements, especially if you are growing in a harsh climate. Growing your plants on a patio is ideal because they are more likely to be in the sun long enough each day and you can still easily get to them.

- Balconies are another option. If your apartment or condo offers one, take full advantage of it. Instead of putting your feet up and sunning there, place a few tables and use the space as your herb garden. This gives your plants plenty of actual access to the sun.

- Sunrooms, including those that are fully enclosed may work as well. They may even be ideal because they are often similar to a greenhouse. They keep temperatures in the space high, with moderate to high humidity and they allow for much more direct sunlight than your windowsill will.

If these are not options you have, consider using the window in your home with the most overall sunlight. Again, measure it. Be sure it is intense light that you are measuring. Choose plants, then, that work well in that environment.

What's the bottom line on sunlight then? Your plants need it. Most will need a very sunny location. If you cannot provide enough light, some herbs may grow, but they will not grow as fully or as quickly as they would otherwise.

Humidity

Don't you hate those days when it is so humid outside you are dripping with sweat? Chances are good you don't keep your home THAT hot either. It wouldn't be good for you or the home. But, what about your herb garden?

Most herbs will need some humidity in the air to grow properly. If you have the air conditioner on full blast, you are pulling out probably too much moisture from the air. So, what are you going to do if plants need humidity and you don't want it?

First, consider how much humidity is ideal for the specific plants you plan to grow. Then, consider this tip when creating your area for herbs. Place a base container on the bottom. Fill this about one layer deep of rocks or other stones. Then, fill the container with water to just cover the stones. This way, the heat in the air will absorb the water and create just enough humidity around the plants to keep them happy.

This way, you do not have to worry about having too much moisture in the air but your plants are not drying out either. Even better, group your herbs together so that you can easily do this in one or two containers. Be careful, though. You do not want the plant's roots to be sitting in water. This will cause damage and it can even cause the death of the plant!
If you do have an area or a method of controlling the humidity in the space, such as in a sunroom, you'll want to aim for a moderate level of humidity in the space. Plants don't need too much humidity - this can be dangerous for mold growth, too.

Temperature

The temperature needs of any plant differ from one to the next. However, plants need warmth, just as humans do. Try putting a potted herb outdoors in 32 degree weather and it will not do well. But, what is the ideal temperature? This depends on a number of factors including the specific type of herb you are growing.

In most cases, it's a good idea to keep the space warm to you. This means a range between 60 and 70 degrees F on average. Most herbs will function well in this environment and will flourish if it is kept consistently at this temperature level.

Since most homes have thermostats, this may seem easy enough to do. However, the proximity to the window, especially on a cold day, can make controlling the temperature around the plant more difficult to do. That's why you'll need to ensure you have a thermometer nearby to monitor the temperature near your plants. Keep the temperature around that range.

Most herbs will tolerate some fluctuation. Usually, you'll want to ensure the temperature remains in the range of 45 degrees and 75 degrees, though. Your plants will not do well in these conditions if you leave them in extreme temperatures for too long. If temperatures get high, use a fan to keep them cool. You may want to consider the use of grow lights if maintaining a high-enough temperature is difficult to do in your herb garden area.

Space

Have you thought about how much space your plants will need? Perhaps not - you are buying seeds or, in some cases, small plants. How much space could they possibly need?

There are two main things to think about when determining how much space you'll need for your plants. First, you need to consider which plants you plan to grow and the size they will be at maturity. Most will do well in a small pot. Others will continue to grow taller and wider. You will have some flexibility in cutting them back, but you'll also find that roots can become very large. Consider the largest size of the plant and then plan for that amount of space in your herb garden for these plants.

The second factor to consider is air circulation. If you have a dozen plants all smashed together in one container, you are going to have problems. You need to ensure there's enough room for good air flow through the area. This will help in keeping the moisture levels under control to avoid the onset of mold. It can also provide you with enough room for the plants to grow and flourish. If there's not enough room for plants to grow outward, you are holding back its growth.

Having just enough space to see the different shapes of each of the plants may be enough. You should be able to see light shining through them, in between them and over the top of each.

Water and Drainage

Finally, you need to consider water. Without it, your plants will die. With too much of it - your plants will die. Water is a necessary component to overall health of the plant. However, too much of it can literally drown the plant. How can you get this right?

First, realize, once again, that every plant's watering needs are different. That means you'll need to spend a little time learning about the plants you plan to grow and their specific needs. However, most plants need good drainage. Even if you are a bit over zealous with the water supply, if you have good drainage, the plants will be able to sustain themselves well. How can you have good drainage?

As mentioned before, using a container under the plants can help. The seeds or plants are put into soil. The soil sits in a pot. The pot needs to have drainage holes under it to allow extra water to flow outward. Of course, this also means that the pot should have something under it to catch that water. One more step to do, though, is to place pebbles or rocks between the pot that the plants are in and the container that will catch the water. You do not want the plants to sit in water. This can cause significant damage to the root system. It can lead to rotting, too.

Once you select the right location for your plants based on all of these factors, you still need to consider the supplies you'll need on hand.

Supplies

When it comes to buying supplies for your plants, don't overdo it. You don't need fancy containers that are over the top, especially if this is your first time. Rather, buy the basics and later, as you become more of a green thumb, you can upgrade to what makes sense for your needs. Still, there are some things you'll need to have available.

Containers

As mentioned previously, it's a good idea to select containers based on the size and needs of the plant. However, you have more options than you may realize.

You can select traditional containers. These would include pots and gardening troughs that allow you to plant more than one plant in them. These are a good option for their affordability. They do require more space than other options, though, which could be a factor for some individuals. It's better, then, to consider a secondary option, such as a vertical garden. You can grow many of the herbs you desire in a vertical garden. Requiring less soil and less room, this can be an ideal option. Hanging by the window, this option can also provide you with significant space saving while providing complete access to the light for plants.

No matter which containers you select, you'll need to ensure they are appropriate for the size and type of plant you plan to grow.

Soil

Soil is very specific for each plant - in some cases. However, if you select an overall quality organic soil, you'll be in a good place. It's a good idea to go with organic only. That's because it will give your plants the best possible chance at growth. The nutrients are better, there are no chemicals, and the substance is all natural - meaning the plants know how to use it. A good quality organic potting soil is likely all you need.

Fertilizer

Do you need fertilizer for the soil? That depends.

In most cases, adding fertilizer is a good thing, if you choose the right type for the plant. There are a few things to consider:

- Additives for soil are best when in liquid form. Others, they do not absorb into the plant well enough.

- Using organic products are best. Do not use any type of chemical-based fertilizer because it will decrease the overall quality of the plants and reduce nutrient levels.

- Don't overdo it. Fertilizers are not always necessary until the soil nutrient levels are reduced.

Follow the directions provided for any product. Too much fertilizer is not always a good thing!

If you have these basic supplies, you are well on your way to having a strong, healthy plant. Of course, you need the seeds or at least the plants first.

Chapter 3: Starting Herbs from Seed

Starting herbs from seed can be a very good thing. It provides some of the best benefits overall. This way, you get a few key benefits:

- You remain in control over what goes into the plant - this includes organic soils and fertilizers. This option gives you the best overall results from that standpoint.

- It does take more work, though. You will need to learn a bit more and to put some extra time into caring for your plants on a regular basis, though this may not be as often as you think.

- You have access to herbs all year round. Though most herbs are seasonal in stores, in their pot form, you can grow them at home any time of the year and pay the same for them as well. That means you'll have no problem having fresh herbs for any meal at any time you want them.

If this sounds like a good idea to you, let's get started. Growing herbs from seed does not have to be as hard as it sounds. Even beginners can do very well at it if they learn a few tips and tricks to doing so.

Gathering What You'll Need

Before you can get started growing herbs from scratch, there are a few more types of items to gather to help you to do so. You do not have to use all of these items, but they can help to provide you with even better results if you do use them.

Here are some things to keep in mind:

- Trays - Trays make it easy for you to plant a large number of plants in an organized, easy to access manner. They may not be the best looking option for your home's decor, but they do add plenty of space. Trays are also a good option to help you to organize and start growing your seeds. They are simply long, lightweight containers divided into spaces for seeds, though some are more open and less confined than others.

- Lights - Do you need lights? If you are planting your seeds out in the open, such as in your greenhouse, you probably do not need any type of grow light. However, if you are serious about growing strong, healthy plants indoors, you'll benefit from one. Plants need the warmth from the light to germinate. That also means that once they begin to get strong, you may not need the growth lights any longer. If you are planning to plant a large number of seeds, this is a good option to consider. Look for specific grow lights as not any light will do.

- Heat pads - As mentioned, growth is an important component to encouraging your seeds to grow. They need the right soil and moisture content, but they also need warmth. Heat pads work easily. They simply are like any other heating pad you may have in your home, creating a soft but warm amount of growth. Keep in mind, though, that this is not the same product as your heating pad for your bank. It's designed to be able to handle a little moisture. Look for these with your other herbal garden growing materials.

Now that you have the basics, it's time to put it all together and to start growing some of the best herbs you've ever had in your life. If that sounds good, you are one-step towards making this work for you.

Before we can get started, though, we need to consider the specific types of seeds you can buy and use. In the next part, we'll break it down by how difficult the plants are to grow from seeds. Though it's possible to grow any of these in your home, you may want to start with some of the basics from the first list before moving on to the more complicated or harder to grow herbs that follow.

Keep in mind, though, that there are various varieties available of most types of herbs. Some may be harder to grow than others are. Some may be super easy in your natural environment whereas others are going to be more of a challenge. Just like any other type of plant you may buy, you will find a variety of species options to consider. What should you look for when buying these seeds:

- Learn the flavor of the plant when fully grown. You will want to choose something that tastes great to you and that is something you are used to.

- Don't be afraid to try something new. If you want to try a different variety, do so.

- Be sure to learn what the specific plant's needs are. Some may require a significantly higher amount of moisture or heat than others do. While this is not necessarily the case for all seeds, some may be more specific or more difficult to grow in certain environments.

- Learn how hard they are to grow. You can find this information from most seed vendors, both online and offline.

It's a good idea to learn as much as you can about the product you are buying. After all, you are investing time and money into this process. You'll want to ensure that you get the best possible results from the hard work you put into it all.

Simple Seeds to Start

Consider the following seeds are easier to start than others are. However, every situation is different. These are some of the most commonly sought after herbs, too. You've likely tried some of them in the past. Let's talk about some options for simple seeds to start with.

Basil

Its freshness spices up any Italian dish, but it's great in both cooked and non-cooked varieties. It's got a lot of flavor and a scent that is simply to die for.

Basil is, perhaps, one of the easiest herbs you will find to grow from seeds. You'll find a wide range of options to choose from, too. Here are some tips for growing basil with success.

- Plant them in cells, such as within a tray, spacing them about two seeds per cell.

- After the plants begin to grow, choose the stronger of the two seedlings from each cell to keep and remove the other.

- You'll want to plant the seeds just under the soil top layer. You should have just a small amount of material on top of them.

- Basil will germinate as soon as four days after planting it.

- Keep the soil moist and warm for the best results. Keep them out of direct sun but in a warm area.

Once the plant begins to grow, you'll notice the leaves forming. As they get two leaves on them, or reach a height of about two inches, you can transplant them into a smaller pot for individual growing. Allow the soil to almost dry out in between watering. Basil does not do well with excessive watering.

Chives and Garlic Chives

Both are full of flavor. Be sure to choose a seed variety that is just that - a strong flavored option. Some versions can be lesser quality and a softer onion flavor. In both cases, chives and garlic chives, the seeds are very fine. Buying quality is important.

Chives and garlic chives are easy to grow from seed. In fact, you don't have to do a lot with them. Ensure the soil in the tray is very loose and fine. It should be easy to sow seeds in, so keep it slightly dry at first. Sow the seeds in the trays and loosely cover with soil.

Both are self-sowing. In other words, you don't need to plant them seed by seed. They will germinate quickly, usually within a few days up to 10 days. Keep the soil moist and dry. The seeds do not need direct sunlight, but the plants, once they begin to get about two inches long will need sunlight to grow fully.

Cilantro

For those that love a Spanish dish or two, there's nothing better than grabbing a bunch of cilantro to add into your mixes or to top onto your dishes. Cilantro can be a fantastic choice when it comes to the flavor. Growing it does not have to be hard to do either.

Cilantro seeds are easy to get to germinate, but you'll need to be careful about where you plant them. You'll find that these herbs do not do well if you have to transplant them. Therefore, it is best simply to sow the seeds in the pots you plan to keep the plants in. Choose a two to three inch deep pot for these.

Cilantro does like the direct sunlight, too. After the seeds start to germinate, you will want to move them into the sun or under lights to grow fully.

To plant seeds, first start by placing the seeds into a container and then allowing them to soak in warm water overnight before you plant them. This will allow the seeds to begin to open up so that when you put them into the soil, they are ready to germinate.

Place the seeds about ¼ inch deep in the soil. Keep the soil moist but not dripping wet. Like most seeds, the soil needs to remain moist but not saturated. Ensure there is a way for water to run off. Cilantro takes about seven to ten days to germinate. At that point, it needs sunlight.

Dill

Who doesn't like the bite and spice that comes from dill? Though you may not use it as readily in your dishes, this is often because it is harder to find in many areas. However, dill works well in salads and in creamy dips. Use it in as many ways as you like, but just give it a taste before you add too much. Some varieties can be strong.

Dill is an easy option for those who are brand new to growing herbs from seeds. They can handle a few mess-ups along the way. The seeds are larger than most other herbs. You'll want to plant them about ½ inch under loose, moist soil. Keep it out of the way of drafts, but still warm. It will take the seeds up to two weeks to germinate, though. Give it time and keep the soil just moist.

Fennel

For those who enjoy the unique taste of fennel, growing it at home is an option. Though it is often thought of as a vegetable, it can be used in the same way as an herb. The anise flavor gives it that distinctive taste, but this herb requires space since it will have a larger bulb on the end.

You'll need well-drained soil that's in full sun throughout the growing period. You'll need containers that are at least 10 inches deep once the seeds sprout and the seedlings get to be about three to four inches in height. Keep seeds spaced out, with no more than a few every few inches as seeds. Later, you'll need to keep the plants about 10 inches apart. Place the seeds into the soil about 1 inch in depth and keep them moist until it is ready to be transplanted.

Oregano

Oregano is a popular choice for pasta dishes but you can use it in much more than sauce. If you are aiming for growing a good amount of oregano, you may want to grow even more and dry it. This herb is an excellent choice for long-term pops of flavor.

Oregano's seeds are small. They also require some patience since it can take between two and three weeks for some varieties to germinate. Once you have a bed of soil for them, simply sprinkle a few of the seeds on the top. Then, use your finger to gently press them just under the oil. Keep them moist but not overly wet. You don't want the soil to remain saturated for long since this can lead to moisture buildup that encourages disease.

Parsley

Parsley, in all of its varieties, is a fresh, wonderful tasting herb. You can add it into any type of salad, but also cook with it. Add it to a pasta sauce or top a taco with it - it is that versatile to use. When it comes to growing parsley, you'll need to have some patience because it, too, takes time to grow. However, it is a fantastic fresh herb to have for dishes or even drinks.

It can take up to four weeks for parsley to germinate. Don't lose sight of the goal, though. A good way to encourage the seeds to open up is to soak them overnight in warm water before planting. Then, plant each one about ¼ of an inch into the moist soil. One more thing to keep in mind is that parsley does not like to be moved. Therefore, you'll want to plant it in the same container you hope to keep it in long term.

Thyme

Is there anything better than the woodsy, charming taste of thyme? You can easily put it into long-cooked dishes, such as roasts and stews, for its flavor enhancing ability. Or, you can chop it up and add it to virtually any dish you are making to give it an earthy taste.

For those who wish to grow thyme from seed, you'll want to ensure you buy a quality, hardy seed. Then, you'll want to take a bit of care with this plant. The seeds are small and it is easy to sow a significant number of them without realizing how many you've planted. You'll want to be careful not to overplant the pot. Be sure to place only a few seeds into the mixture of soil. You just need about two to four seeds in one cell or pot. Use your finger to press them into the soil, but no more than ½ inch in. It can take up to three weeks for the seedlings to begin to grow. You'll want to keep the soil damp and the plants in direct sunlight once they start to grow.

Intermediate Seeds to Grow

This set of herbs is a bit more challenging, but they are all still good options for those who want to start growing herbs at home. You'll want to spend a bit more time ensuring that this process is done properly as these plants are slightly less forgiving than others are. Still, even beginners should be okay with a few helpful tips.

Anise

Anise has a strong flavor, similar to that of licorice. If you love that tang and want it, adding it to any of your dishes including stews, soups or sometimes salads, you'll want to grow this plant from seed. The plants themselves can get to be as tall as two feet, so you'll need to have enough room for them to grow. This herb does not like to be transplanted so be sure to sow the seeds in the pot you plan to keep it in for the long term.

Be sure it has good drainage, too, since you do not want the seeds sitting in water for too long. Plant the seeds all over the top of the soil mixture. Then, cover with about ¼ of an inch of more soil, pushing down on the soil afterwards. In a larger pot, you can easily plant six to eight seeds with ease. Keep the soil wet by using a spray bottle. You'll also want to keep the temperature in the 60 to 70 degree range to encourage growth. The anise seeds will germinate within two weeks.

Borage

It's a beautiful flower, but a tasty herb, too. Borage is a nice choice to add to a glass of lemonade in the summer months or teas in the wintertime. These plants grow to be about three feet tall, but they are not too difficult to grow.

It will tolerate some partial shade, though it will do better in full sun after the seedlings germinate. You'll want to ensure the soil remains moist. Plant the seeds just under the surface of the soil. You can plant a number of seeds in a small area, but you will need to thin them out as they begin to grow. It can take about two weeks for germination to happen.

Chervil

Chervil is a softer type of herb, one that has a slight licorice like taste to it, but not in an overpowering way. It is an excellent type of herb that will also add a pop of color to your herb garden with its beautiful purple flowers. The plant will grow to about one foot in height, in some cases can be much taller.

Use a rich soil that has a good amount of moisture locking ability. It takes seeds about two weeks to germinate. Within a month of that, you'll be able to pick the leaves to use in your dishes. When planting, keep the depth of the seeds shallow, only about ½ inch under the surface of the soil. Tap into place. Keep the soil moist and well-drained. The seedlings will want direct light once they rise out of the soil.

Cumin

Cumin has a smoky taste to it. The plant will grow tall but thin. Keep in mind, you'll grow it for the seeds it produces – cumin seeds are the best component of this plant. These seeds occur right after the pink and white flowers arrive.

To grow cumin from seed, sow directly into the soil they will stay in since it does not do well as a transplant. It can take about 90 days until you get to the point of harvest, but the plants will germinate within two to three weeks, sometimes longer. You'll want to grow a lot of plants to make enough seed to use readily. The good news is that the plant does better when it's crowded.

It will need damp conditions and full sunlight. Sprinkle seeds on top of a bed of soil and then cover with about ¼ inch more of soil.

Lemon Balm

A flavorful additive to any herb garden, lemon balm should be one you add in. It is a type of mint that you can use in cooked dishes or fresh. It makes a great option for those who want something with bright flavor that's easy to grow.

To grow lemon balm, use a vermiculite and potting soil mixture. You'll want to ensure the soil is damp but not dripping wet. Then, place the seeds about ¼ of an inch into the soil by pushing them in with your finger. Mist the top of the soil throughout the growing period until the seedlings grow. You'll need to keep the herb in warm air but not in direct sunlight. It can take up to three weeks to see germination take place. You may need to think about the seedlings or you can transplant them to larger pots when they are about three to four inches in height. Keep these plants about 12 inches apart to allow them to grow well. You can pick the leaves to begin using them as soon as they reach about six to eight inches in height or have more than a dozen leaves.

Marjoram

Marjoram could become your favorite houseplant. At least, it will like being indoors as long as the temperature is high enough. It is often used in French cuisine but you'll be able to use it in many dishes when you want a sweeter herb. You can keep this one right on your windowsill as long as there is enough light.

To grow it, you'll need to sow the seeds in average or better soil. They will tolerate some dry conditions since they come from arid regions. Place the seeds about ½ inch under the soil. Keep the seeds warm and moist until they germinate. As they grow, water them once or twice a week, but not much more. Do not use any fertilizer here because this will change the flavor significantly and not always in a good way. The flowers need to be picked as soon as they grow. You can harvest the leaves once the plant has about two dozen or more leaves. Younger leaves have the best flavor.

Peppermint and Spearmint

Who doesn't enjoy a cup of mint tea or a bright additive for a salad or soup? Peppermint and spearmint are two of the best options. They are found throughout Mediterranean cooking, but work in dishes from around the world. These bright green leaves are grown on a bushy plant. Once you plant it and it does well, mint will come back year after year, which makes it the ideal choice for any indoor garden. Also, in containers, there is no worry of the plants spreading invasively.

Sow the seeds directly into the pot that the plant will remain in as this will give the best overall outcome. Use about two to three seeds per cell. Place them about ½ inch under the moist soil and keep it that way until the seeds grow. Warmth is important. Once the seedlings grow, thin them back so that there is only one plant every eight to 12 inches. It does well in partial shade or full sun. Be sure the soil drains well. Once the seedlings are about six inches in height the leaves will begin to grow. You can pick the leaves at any time after about a dozen are present on the plant.

Sage

Sage is a very earthy herb. It has a lot of flavor, but it is not the type of herb that will overpower a dish. You can use it in long-cooked dishes, or use it in a more fresh form. You'll want to have some patience when growing this plant, though.

Sage likes to grow slowly. That means you'll want to give it time. The seeds are about average in size. Plant them about ½ inch into the soil. Keep the soil moist with good drainage. You'll also want to keep it warm to generate some activity. It can take up to three weeks for the sage sprouts to begin to show up out of the soil. As long as the soil remains evenly moist, they will germinate eventually.

Tarragon (French)

Tarragon is commonly used in French cooking, but this plant is a good option for any type of earthy meal. It does best in dry and barren soils, making it an easier plant to grow for those who do not want to have to watch it every day. The plant will get to be between two and five feet in height, depending on the variety you select. The leaves have a strong smell to them and add to the freshness of any dish.

To grow tarragon, put it in the worst soil you have - as long as it is soil not just clay or sand. It will need full sun to do well, though. Mix some sand or gravel into the soil as well. Keep the environment dry rather than moist. You'll want to sow the seeds about ½ inch into the soil. Then, allow the seedlings to grow and thin them out as necessary. They will need about a foot in between each plant eventually.

Once the plant begins to grow, they do not require much attention from you at all. You can harvest and dry the leaves out if you want or use them fresh. Keep the soil slightly dry throughout the growing period.

Challenging Herbs to Grow From Seed

Some seeds are harder to grow. Why is this? It could be because the herbs take more time or they require more patience. It's also important to point out that some herbs just do not grow as well or as easily as others do, especially in containers. They take more time, require different amounts of soil nutrients or they are just not that dependable.

If you want to grow any of these herbs, and by all means you should, give it a try. You'll want to put some extra time into ensuring that the herb seeds you pick are high in quality and that you learn as much as you can about the specific growing requirements of the seeds. This can make all of the difference in your success.

Bay

Bay is a fantastic herb to have in your home because it provides a wide range of uses. It has a strong flavor in the dried form, but in the fresh form it is significantly softer. Use it in longer cooking dishes for the best option. When it comes to growing bay, remember, it's a tree rather than a small plant and requires more room indoors. Look for varieties that are dwarf or smaller to ensure you are getting the right product.

The seeds need to be kept warm while germinating, so use a heating mat if possible. You don't want to keep the soil saturated either. It can take from ten days (very few varieties) up to several months to see germination happen. It may be best to grow this one from cuttings rather than seed. As soon as you begin to see the leaves sprouting, thin the seedlings if needed. Plant it in individual containers. You will need to maintain the tree as it grows, trimming it back. You can harvest from it as soon as a large number of leaves, at least two dozen, have developed.

Chamomile

When it comes to enjoying a refreshing cup of herbal tea, chamomile may be one of the best choices available. It has a sweet smell, beautiful daisy-like flowers, and a softer flavor. It is a great choice for a variety of different uses including in floral teas, drinks, and dishes. The leaves do have a slightly bitter taste.

To grow this herb, you'll want to plan for a good deal of space since they can grow as high as 30 inches, though varieties do have different heights. You can grow them in individual containers on your windowsill, though. You don't even need to put these in direct sunlight.

Chamomile seeds are sprinkled over an area of soil and then depressed just slightly into the soil. It's best to use a rich soil- one that has added nutrients. Keep the soil moist, too. If you want to encourage the seedlings to grow to a fuller plant, you can use a fertilizer on them, but only use a water-based fertilizer.

It can take two weeks or longer for the plants to sprout to seedlings, but it is well worth waiting for. You'll be able to harvest the plants when the flowers peak in bloom. Be sure that you pick the leaves and then allow them to dry out so they last longer or you can use them fresh.

Lavender

For a wonderful flavor and a nice scent, try lavender in your herbal garden. In fact, it has been used for centuries for a fresh scent as well as for various food applications. Though it is not an easy plant to grow, it is definitely one that is worth the bit of extra attention you put into it.

Sow the seeds into a bed of soil. You will likely need to thin them later. Eventually, they will need to be about 18 inches apart. It's best to keep lavender in the sun once the seeds begin to grow, but keep the seeds out of drafts while they are germinating. It can take a good deal of time for germination to occur, but using grow lights can definitely speed things up and it can also create a fuller plant. Ensure you keep the soil moist, but well drained throughout the growing period.

You can harvest the plants in all forms, including the leaves, stems and flowers. It's best to harvest in the early morning when the oils in the leaves are strongest.

Rosemary

Rosemary has an incredible taste and it can work well in virtually application. The wood stems are removed and the fine, thin leaves are chopped and used in numerous dishes. It's a good idea to use them in roasts or other long-cooked dishes.

The challenge is that rosemary isn't the easiest plant to grow. In fact, it can take six weeks or longer for germination to occur and even then, only 25 to 50 percent of the seeds will actually take. That's why you'll want to soak the seeds overnight in warm water before trying to plant them. Using a propagation mat can help too. Cover the seedbed with a light coating of seeds and then add about ¼ inch of soil on top.

Keep the soil slightly moist and ensure good drainage. These plants will be okay with dry soil, but be sure to water them well if they look like they are wilting. Once the bush reaches a couple of feet, you'll want to trim it up. You can store the leaves, on the stem, in a freezer for when you need them.

Stevia

Stevia has become one of the best natural sugar substitutes available. This plant is an all-natural solution to those who want a healthy way to sweet drinks or dishes. It can work well in deserts, too. The leaves are where the sweetness is and remember, this is a calorie-free and carb-free way of getting the sweet craving you have met.

Stevia naturally grows in the sub-tropics. That's what makes it more difficult to grow elsewhere. However, it can do well as an annual in some conditions, even those areas that frost, so long as it is given the right nutrients.

The seeds are hard to germinate. In fact, you may find that the seed germination rates are very low. This only means you'll want to sow more seeds at one time. It's best to keep the soil moist to encourage germination and, like other seeds that are difficult to get growing, you can soak them in warm water for a few hours to encourage it.

The best way to get seeds to sprout and then to grow is to keep the soil temperature up at about 65 degrees or slightly higher. It's a good idea to use a germination mat or a heater to do this. Once the plants do sprout and begin to grow several inches tall, you'll need to thin them as needed and then plant them six to eight inches apart. Do not allow the plants to sit in overly damp soil, but keep the soil moist.

Chapter 4: Buying Plants

If growing herbs from seeds sounds like too much work, don't worry. There's another option available to you. You can and should consider buying plants and growing the herbs in your home this way. Buying plants is a very good option, although the ability variety may be limited, especially outside of the normal growing season. It takes less time to get healthy herbs in your kitchen to begin using and it also takes a lot of the work out of the job. However, there are some things you need to keep in mind.

What to Look For

Know your grower. Don't buy off the grocery store's shelves when you want a quality plant that has plenty of freshness. Rather, find a grower that specializes in herbs. Then, consider the following.

- Is the plant certified organic? If not, that means pesticides or other chemicals were used in the creation of the plants.

- Is the plant super green or very healthy looking? That's usually due to chemical fertilizers used to make the plants last longer on store shelves. It's not good for overall quality especially since fertilizers like this (chemical based products) become an addiction to the plant. Plants don't thrive without it once they are given it.

- Find out the variety of the plant you are buying. Just like buying seeds, there are various flavor, appearance, and scent differences between plants. You'll want to put some time into learning which varieties you want and then to find a grower offering them.

- Learn about the grower or vendor, too. You'll want to find out if they grow the plants themselves, how they ship them and what other people find good or bad about the company. This can make a big difference in the overall quality of the product. You need to know if you are buying quality.

- Read the needs of the plant. Though you should pick a variety that you want to enjoy, remember that each variety has specific needs. What amount of sunlight does it need? What amount of space will it require both now and well into the future as it begins to grow and bloom? How much attention do you need to give it once it is at home? And, what amount of heat or moisture control does the plant require to do well? You need this information in order to grow a healthy plant.

Don't just buy what's available but do some research to ensure that the plants you are buying are worth it. Moreover, be sure to keep in mind the overall appearance of the plant. If it has any of the concerns listed in the next chapter, pass on it. You'll want a healthy looking plant that has plenty of strong life in it. It really does pay off.

If you don't want to worry about starting from scratch, buying plants makes sense. It's also a good option for those plants that are harder to grow or those that may take a long time to germinate. This way, you can cut to the chase and have great herbs nearly ready to go when you are ready to. That can make all of the difference in the overall quality.

Chapter 5: Solving Problems

Plants, no matter if they are started from seeds or if you buy them, may have problems from time to time. It's best to know the variety well and to ensure that you are buying the highest quality seeds or plants from your vendor. Aside from that, you'll want to react to any type of problem that arises while you are growing and caring for your herbs. There are several things to keep in mind no matter what concerns you have.

Pests

Pests are a problem inside and outside of the home. Leave a small army of pests to your herbs and within a few days you may have nothing left. It is best to keep an eye on your plants on an ongoing basis. That means you need to look for any signs of problems. By simply caring for your plants on a regular basis, you will be able to spot problems as they occur. React quickly. Here are some things to keep in mind.

Aphids, mealy bugs, mites, and whiteflies tend to be the most common type of pests that affect indoor herbs. However, there are others that can get in and do damage.

- Outdoors, these pests are less of a problem because predators will keep them at bay and they do offer nutrients to the soil while also loosening dirt. In the house, they are not welcome.

- You can use a mild soap to wash off most plants. Do this in the sink and simply rinse them off, being careful not to upset the roots much and to wash off any soap from the leaves without allowing it to get into the soil.

- Pick off bugs as you see them. Though this is not necessarily the easiest option, but does work when you just notice a small problem. Its best to do this instead of trying to dig up the plant.

- If it is hot outside, it's a good idea to put the plant outside for a few days. This is only an option in the summer when the plant will thrive in those conditions. You will want to ensure the plant is still maintained properly.

- Finally, you can use an organic pesticide if the problem is significant or infestation has occurred on numerous plants in your herbal garden. It pays to use a quality, organic product rather than any chemical-based product.

If you notice a specific problem reoccurring, find out what type of pest it is and target specific treatments for it.

Disease

Another problem for many herbs is disease. We've already talked about what happens when the soil is too moist - this can lead to rotting of the soil, plant and the seeds. However, diseases can happen for many reasons.

Generally, plants cry out to you that there's a problem. They do this simply by showing evidence of the problem, such as leaves that look weaker and a less green color. Sometimes, you'll notice a milky white substance on the leaves or on the roots. It's a good idea to not brush off these problems and to take action as soon as possible to correct the problem.

Here are some tips for dealing with diseases.

- Determine what the problem is and correct it. For example, if the plant is limp and looks week, it may be not getting enough sunlight. Move it into full sun or use a growers lamp on it for a few days.

- If the problem is that the plant seems to be less green then consider the soil. If the herb has been sitting in the same soil for a long time, it may have depleted the nutrients it needs. Some herbs tolerate replanting and others do not. In cases that they do not, use a water-based fertilizer to boost the nutrient content.

- If the soil is too wet, this can lead to rotting. Try to replace some of the over-wet soil with looser, drier soil. Be sure there is ample drainage in the plant - this means having accessible holes that allow water to escape.

- If the plant is not getting enough sun, you'll want to move it. In some cases, you may need to turn on that grow light. Some plants may begin to wilt if they are in the sun or under the grow light too long. Not only should you flip it off and provide partial shade, but you should also spend time watering and misting the leaves to bring the temperature down.

In some cases, you may need to remove the deadened portions of the plant. This may include cutting off a portion of a rotting root bulb or trimming away stalks, stems or leaves that seem to be isolated and dying. This can help to stop the plant from trying to use its energy to repair the problem and instead allows it to keep growing.

Again, it's best if you put a bit of time into finding the root of the problem specifically and then applying the proper treatment of the condition. Often, you can find great pictures and help online for doing so.

Tips for Avoiding Problems

As your herbal garden is growing and developing, there are steps you can take to minimize the problems and to get better overall results. The following are some basic "rules" to follow to ensure this is the case.

1. Never overwater your plants. In nearly all cases, soil should be kept moist but not soggy. Always have good drainage available and be sure to check the drainage holes under your plant to ensure water can still flow outwards. When it comes to light moisture, instead of using any type of watering can, use a spray bottle with water in it instead.

2. Don't think fertilizer is always a good thing. Too much fertilizer will burn your plants. Specifically, nitrogen can cause infestations and it can lead to damage to the roots. It's best to use a quality, organic soil mixture and then to fertilize only once or twice a year as needed.

3. Don't use chemicals of any sort, if possible. As mentioned, these products cause the plant to become dependent on them.

4. If you notice a problem and cannot figure out the cause, it may be best to repot the plant. This can help to give the plant a new start, especially when you use new soil. Just be sure to remove as much of the soil present before replanting.

5. When it comes to trimming and using your herbs, try to wait until the plant has ample leaves before removing any. This is, after all, the plant's method for growing and taking in nutrients from the

sun. You don't want just one serving of the herbs, after all, but ongoing access to them.

6. Sunlight is the big factor. Most plants benefit from sunlight. Some will tolerate indirect sunlight. It's usually a good idea to ensure plants get a few hours of sunlight each day otherwise they simply may not grow well. However, remember that every variety is different.

7. If you have significant problems with the stem, crown or the root, then it may be best to let go of the plant before it infests other plants nearby to it. This is a critical step in ensuring that the plants don't catch the problem.

If you invest the time into them, herbs can last for years. Though this varies based on the specific plant variety, it's possible to maintain herbs for a long time with regular care. Even better, it's always a good idea to try something new, grow a new batch of plants or to simply get a fresh start. Herbs can fill your home with plenty of great tastes, smells and lots of great reasons to cook. In fact, with them available, you may want to cook more often than you do now.

Chapter 6: Resources to Use

There are dozens of providers of herbal growing products and resources. As long as you do some quick research to find out what they are offering and what their policies are, try them out.

You will find that it's better to use online resources or a good vendor locally to buy from rather than buying from home improvement stores. You need quality if you want these plants to thrive and to be excellent additions to your home. Most of these locations only offer options for the outdoors - there is a difference for those who want to grow herbs indoors.

Seed and Supply Vendors

The following are some sources of seed vendors worth investing in. Take into consideration a few options. These are just options - do your own research on which is the best based on what you hope to buy and grow in your home.

- Native Seeds - http://nativeseeds.org/ This organization is a very good one. It is a non-profit organization that promote seed conservation. Request a catalog and check out the huge selection of options.

- Burpee - http://www.burpee.com/ - It is one of the largest organizations selling seeds in the United States and North America overall. The quality is good and the selection is also ideal. You'll find a wide range of seeds and plants you can buy directly from this company. You'll also find all of your seed supplies here.

- Baker Creek Heirloom Seeds - http://rareseeds.com/ - The quality here is good and that's perhaps the most important consideration. The company features heirloom seeds which can be more expensive, but may be worth it.

- Harris Seeds - http://www.harrisseeds.com - This company has a wide range of options to choose from, including a number of worldwide products. The information on the site is good, too. You'll find most of what you need available at a good price.

- Mountain Rose Herbs - http://www.mountainroseherbs.com -

The company offers a line of medicinal herb seeds that may be perfect for those who want a higher quality plant for herbal remedies. The company also offers certified organic products.

- Johnny's Selected Seeds - http://www.johnnyseeds.com/ - A wide range of options and all of the tools and supplies you need are available here. The company is employee-owned, which is nice because it means the quality is good. Look for the organic products available.

Buy quality, plant wisely, and use your herbs. They are definitely worth the effort it takes to grow them and your whole home will appreciate them.

More by Julia Winchester

If you enjoyed this book, you might consider checking out my other books:

Microgreens: A Beginner's Guide to the Benefits of Cultivation and Consumption (http://www.amazon.com/gp/product/B009SB9C3I/)

Wheatgrass: Growing and Juicing for Better Nutrition (http://www.amazon.com/gp/product/B00AF3FMSM/)

Both are available as both paperback and Kindle versions through Amazon.com.

15650022R00024

Printed in Great Britain
by Amazon